THE REPUBLIC OF
MOTHERHOOD

THE REPUBLIC OF MOTHERHOOD

Liz Berry

Chatto & Windus
LONDON

For T & T, with love

9 10

Chatto & Windus, an imprint of Vintage,
20 Vauxhall Bridge Road,
London SW1V 2SA

Chatto & Windus is part of the Penguin Random House group of companies whose addresses can be found at global.penguinrandomhouse.com.

 Penguin
Random House
UK

First published by Chatto & Windus in 2018

penguin.co.uk/vintage

A CIP catalogue record for this book is available from the British Library

ISBN 9781784742676

Typeset in 10/13 pt Minion
by Integra Software Services Pvt. Ltd, Pondicherry

Printed and bound in Great Britain by Clays Ltd, Elcograf S.p.A.

Penguin Random House is committed to a sustainable future for our business, our readers and our planet. This book is made from Forest Stewardship Council® certified paper.

Contents

The Republic of Motherhood

I crossed the border into the Republic of Motherhood
and found it a queendom, a wild queendom.
I handed over my clothes and took its uniform,
its dressing gown and undergarments, a cardigan
soft as a creature, smelling of birth and milk,
and I lay down in Motherhood's bed, the bed I had made
but could not sleep in, for I was called at once to work
in the factory of Motherhood. The owl shift,
the graveyard shift. Feedingcleaninglovingfeeding.
I walked home, heartsore, through pale streets,
the coins of Motherhood singing in my pockets.
Then I soaked my spindled bones
in the chill municipal baths of Motherhood,
watching strands of my hair float from my fingers.
Each day I pushed my pram through freeze and blossom
down the wide boulevards of Motherhood
where poplars bent their branches to stroke my brow.
I stood with my sisters in the queues of Motherhood –
the weighing clinic, the supermarket – waiting
for its bureaucracies to open their doors.
As required, I stood beneath the flag of Motherhood
and opened my mouth although I did not know the anthem.
When darkness fell I pushed my pram home again,
by lamp-light wrote urgent letters of complaint
to the Department of Motherhood but received no response.
I grew sick and was healed in the hospitals of Motherhood
with their long-closed isolation wards
and narrow beds watched over by a fat moon.

The doctors were slender and efficient
and when I was well they gave me my pram again
so I could stare at the daffodils in the parks of Motherhood
while winds pierced my breasts like silver arrows.
In snowfall, I haunted Motherhood's cemeteries,
the sweet fallen beneath my feet –
Our Lady of the Birth Trauma, Our Lady of Psychosis.
I wanted to speak to them, tell them I understood,
but the words came out scrambled, so I knelt instead
and prayed in the chapel of Motherhood, prayed
for that whole wild fucking queendom,
its sorrow, its unbearable skinless beauty,
and all the souls that were in it. I prayed and prayed
until my voice was a nightcry,
sunlight pixellating my face like a kaleidoscope.

Connemara

I stepped out of my skin
that dusk in Connemara
where bush crickets thrummed
like pylons
and the lane smelled
of tar and clover.
What lay beneath
was fragile, not yet
ready for its season.
The drizzle
made sore music
of my nerve ends.
I was beautiful to the crows
as a butcher's window.

In the vespers I was glorious,
so raw I felt each mote.
Kites beheld
my glowing jellyfish brain.
My heart was carmine,
radiant as a saint
in a wayside shrine.
I raised my arms
to the sky
and the air kissed me
with its stinging
worshipful mouth.

I threw the skin to the wind,
sweet sack
I'd tended and punished
for thirty-three years.
Now moths would make
heaven of it.
Let them come,
I thought,
I am ready.
Inside me you pulsed,
single celled,
extraordinary.

Horse Heart

It's a stable in here:
the sodden hay of broken waters,
each of us private and lowing in our stalls
while all night, from the monitors,
the sound of babies' hearts like hooves
stumbling   stamping
through our bodies
into the high wet grass of their lives.

How reckless they are –
lost now   then again
in snowy fields of static.
Too fast and they're gone, too slow
and they might never reach us at all
but fall, heads crowned by vetch
and dandelion, noses cold
to the belly of earth.

Oh these horse nights,
darkless nights, the endless running
of the herd, fear a hoof
upon my chest.
I lie in my sweats and beckon you up.
Little horse heart, foal,
let my love be your paddock, your bridle,
your trough.

Transition

When the fires swept   lit my body ablaze
I wanted to crawl into that lake at Kejimakujik
silent star-mirroring lake   so deep
it knows no grave   no soul
slip my flesh   and slither loose   an eel
clot-dark and sinewy   skin the sheen of the lake
of the night the lake swallowed
an arrow of blood   quivering
through the water   loveless   childless
my storm-lantern jaw swinging in the black
unblinking eyes reflecting black
seed pearl teeth singing only of black
black so black   it stunned my heart
and spangled my mind like an electric bolt.

The Visitation

Eloise, I opened too soon, a foxglove, on that papered bed,
my waters sweet and grassy as the cut-side at dawn,
and cried when the little nurse drew the curtains around me

saying "hush wench, yo've a long night ahead" and left me
to watch the sun tumble and climb through high gridded windows.
In the cubicles around me women were sobbing.

I lay my cheek against the cold bars of the trolley
as my body clenched and unfurled and I slept for just a moment
and in that moment I was fourteen again, still your girl,

lying on my back on the playing fields in Dudley,
blue school skirt hitched, the unmown grass wet
against my thighs; summer overspilling, everything loosened.

You knelt before me, your scent of hairspray and menthol
kaylighing my lungs, took my face in your palms,
placed a crown of daisies in my hair and held me down

until I bloomed, my mouth spilling flowers, feverish
through the fodes and gardens, donkey-bites and alleys,
the dolls-house terraces where girls dreamt.

I knew the time had come to yield like a meadow
so I did, love, and you moved through me like the May breeze
and I was blessed.

Sky Birth

Bringing you to the world, I let the mountain enter me:
mauve, shadow, the sky a zoetrope spinning crows
   and rain-soaked fog.
I let in the scree and nodding heads of heather,
a path hidden by moss
where waymarkers of dotterel skulls whistled in the breeze.
I opened my chest to the wind,
        which soughed and howled
over the voice of the midwife, the beeping monitors.

The ascent was steep,
              dirt and stream, the air electrified
with concentration. A hare leapt in the milkweed,
mizzle fell
     slant on my spine.
Up   up   I climbed until I could no longer see
the bottom, the place I had begun
but retched with the heights, poor beast of the base world.

Up up.   Higher.   Further.
I cried out but the gale swallowed it and sang back my name
until everything was burning,
until the face was sheer and the rush were on fire,
the bones of death gleaming beneath.

      I knelt on all fours, scrambled, desperate
     to reach the summit, the splitting peak –
        when it came it came fast, a shining crown

through the slap of the storm,
        for a second we were alone on that highest place
            and love, oh love,
                        I would have gladly left my body
        on that lit ledge for birds to pick clean
for my heart was in yours now
and your small body would be the one to carry us.

Bobowler

Darkling herald,
see her flower-face on a waning moon
and spake her name aloud
to conjure the voice
of one you loved and let slip
through the wing gauze of jeth.

In the owl-light,
when loneliness shines
through your bones like a bare bulb,
she'll come for you,
little psyche bringing missives
from the murmuring dark.

She comes to all the night birds:
cuckoos, thieves, the old uns
and the babbies in their dimlit wums,
the boy riding his bike
up Beacon Hill, heart thundering
like a strange summer storm.

And the messages she carries
in her slow soft flight?
Too tender to speak of, too heartsore,
but this: I am waiting.
The love that lit the darkness between us
has not been lost.

The Yellow Curtains

The colour is repellent. A smouldering unclean yellow,
strangely faded by the slow-turning sunlight.
For seventy-three days I have lain here.
Carmine on goldenrod. Toile de jouy.
A shepherdess bowing before an archer,
a skittish hart watchful by the brook.
Seventy-three nights *on this great immovable bed*
whilst inside me the careful work never ceases:
brain tissue, marrow, a coppice of lungs
leafing and tossing in the swell.
I haven't felt like writing before, since that first day –
But I must not think about that.
These curtains have shut out the Summer;
the silver birch undressing, her leaves
a snowstorm; frost feathering the glass.
I am alone a good deal just now
and I cry at nothing and cry most of the time,
in the cock-crow, through the chiming hours,
the velvet meadows of my dream life.
There are things in these curtains
that nobody knows but me or ever will.
The small face in the oaks. *Blessed little goose.*
She reaches to me, calls for me. Mama.
But I dare not move, dare not sit up,
for in that mint-green ward
there are ventilators, defibrillators, needles
for tiny veins like scraps of red thread.

No. *It is the strangest yellow!*
It makes me think of all the yellow things
I ever saw – not beautiful ones like buttercups
but old foul, bad yellow things.
How many minutes now, how many days?
This toil of joy. *He said I was his darling*
and his comfort and all he had, and that I must
take care of myself. For his sake.
I can stand it so much easier than a baby, you see.
But I cry at nothing and cry most of the time.
At the swollen breast of the shepherdess.
At the little face in the oaks, darling
little face. Dear god, how I love you
in darkness, you small pulsing creature.
For seventy-three days now. Smouldering.
Yellow. *I don't know why I should write this.*
I don't want to. I don't feel able.

So Tenderly It Wounds Them

On mornings mute as the blackbird's bride
I hear the bones of the new mothers   singing
from their lamp-lit houses   through rain-rattled streets
their hair hanging loose   their hearts violet
as the centre of the flame   so furious the burning.

Sweet ghosts   who've been awake
with their babies through the dark
kneeling to the filth and holy rags of the body
so tenderly it wounds them.
Who rise from grey light to walk the wet streets –

their tiny saints adrift in sleep's brackish waters –
or weep through rain-blurred windscreens
wearing love as a winter coat   a baby dozing
in the backseat. Who are lonely
though never alone

in the playgroup   living room
steam-windowed cafe. Who find a trinket
from the old country – a photograph   train ticket –
and press it to their keening breasts
like a relic.

Who catch each other's wrists
in the clinic   by the endless swings   whispering
I never knew it would be like this but God when he laughs ...

and their joy is a kite   cut loose
from its strings.

Wind-blown girls   changed
beyond all knowing   like young trees in spring
blossom to fall   now bowed and rustled
by every small breath.
In the blood-pink of morning

punched out by love   I lie
with my child and hear them singing
flesh pulp sinew soul   I hear them
I hear myself   our dark soft moans
animals waking in a starless country dawn.

Early

There are times we're like new sweethearts,
awake through the shining hours, close
as spoons in the polishing cloth of dawn,
or sombre winter mornings,
the terrace a diorama:
bare poplar, yellow window, a woman
rocking a baby in her arms.
I tell you things I've never told
another creature, strange lullabies
like the purling of larks, winging up
into the withdrawing dark.
In the early light,
every line I wanted to write for you
seems already written, read
and forgotten
so I sing the secret part, my true one,
of being born again
as you were born,
of kissing your mouth in the hospital,
love-sick, cut, stitched, undone
and forgiving you for everything
your sweet love would thieve me of.

Placenta

Some women eat theirs but I buried mine
    beneath the black waters at Wren's Nest
with a steel shovel and my bare fingers
    delivered it back to the subterranean fires.
It was a gorgeous fecund thing   mechanical
    but carnal   veined like a beast's heart
it smeared my hands burgundy   my mouth
    with the starry gut-punch of our first kiss.
Blood oblation   the weight of it knocked
    the breath from me. When I cradled it
above its grave it was crawling with jewels
    trilobites and brachiopods   blinking eyes
which saw only briny hot darkness and flood
    upon flashing flood of creation.
The land moaned as I knelt   parting her seams
    the chamber within soot and pearl.
I spoke his name and spat on the plot.

Marie

I didn't know when we met
in the Baptist church hall
that you would save my soul

Marie, with your black hair,

that I would walk through sleet
with my pram to your door,
my heart clem-gutted

Marie, with your black hair,

and you'd be waiting
with your curtains pulled
and the flame blue

Marie, with your black hair,

take my hands in yours
and touch the palms
saying *I know I know*

Marie, with your black hair,

you could see I was drowning
and taking him with me,
my boy, my baby,

Marie, with your black hair,

you made a wave of your body,
and like a gasping fish
I was borne upon it.

The Spiritualist Church

I've never spoken to anyone of this –
the Spiritualist church, its squat brick body,
the mossy wall where snails congregate
in worshipful hundreds on wet dusks.
Every day that first winter,
the winter I thought would bury us both,
I walked past that church in sallow light
carrying my son at my chest,
my bones luminous with tiredness.
I'd stand at the gates and read
the inscription on the sign
      Light   Nature   Truth
drawing it into my mouth like anaesthetic
until I believed it was a message for me
to ascend like a dove through the red roofs
or sow myself into the sod.
      When the snow fell
I thought it was snowing inside my body,
milk turning to ice in my breasts,
snow piling sullen in the crib
of my pelvis. The air burnt my lungs
and I was back on a trolley in the mint room,
frozen from the waist down,
certain he was dying, that I was letting him
die and they were cutting me open –
      When the sky was dolorous
with sleet, I stood at the gates and dreamt

of begging them to take us in,
to lift my baby from my arms
and lay me down in a room of shadows
so I could shut my eyes at last and the hush
would cover me like a burial sheet
and someone gentle would rest their palms on me,
touch me with a light so staggering
I'd be opened up, my soul rising
from the x-ray of my skeleton
like a white-veined moth, my body below
hollow as an instrument, humming
with voices: women in darkness,
women with babies, down on their knees
in smothering houses, standing
on bridges, coats loosened to wings,
all of them uttering, murmuring at once: *I see you.*
Now understand, that love can take this shape –
a dove plummeting through white-sleeved night,
that this is a healing, a laying on of hands.

Lullaby

Babby, the sky's turning collied as coal.
Tom Robin's gone nesting
now bobowler's testing
his wings for his flight to our cobwebby bulb.

And the moon is a penny tossed into the cut
to pay for the dream boat that ferries us off.

So hush now, my sweet chick,
Hush yo, hush hush.

Darlin, the night is a randan o' dreams:
owd wammels am howling
at ghost cats who'm prowling
for long eaten rots in the rafters and beams.

And the moon is a penny tossed into the cut
to pay for the dream boat that ferries us off.

Lovey, the night is as deep as the thick
where restless black osses
still stamp for their bosses
to lead 'em back wum from the gob o' the pit.

And the moon is a penny tossed into the cut
to pay for the dream boat that ferries us off.

Listen, the song o' the night's falling soft:
oak trees am shushing
the homers who'm rushing
to roost in the tumbly snug o' their lofts.

And the moon is a penny tossed into the cut
to pay for the dream boat that ferries us off.

Oh babby, in Tipton, from Lye to Blackheath,
our dark towns doze under
their blankets o' slumber;
so curl in my crook, let me lull you to sleep.

For the moon is a penny tossed into the cut
to pay for the dream boat that ferries us off.

So hush now, my sweet chick,
Hush yo, hush hush.

The Steps

And this is where it begins, love –
you and I, alone one last time in the slatey night,
the smell of you like autumn, soil and bonfire,
that November the fourth feeling inside us.
There can be no truer wedding than this:
your bare hand in mine, my body winded
with pain, as you lead me to the car, to the
soon life. And we are frightened, so frightened –

Who will we be when we come back?
Will we remember ourselves?
Will we still touch each other's faces
in the darkness, the white noise of night
spilling over us, and believe there is nothing
we could not know or love?

Glossary

bobowler moth
clem-gutted starved or miserable
collied black and sooty
cuckoos sweethearts
cut canal
donkey-bite small patch of rough ground
fode backyard
homers homing pigeons
jeth death
kaylighing intoxicating
osses horses
randan riot
rots rats
spake speak
the thick Black Country coal seam
wammels dogs
wum home

Acknowledgements

Thanks to the editors of the anthologies and journals in which several of these poems first appeared: *Best Friends Forever, The Compass, The Emma Press Anthology of Motherhood, Granta, The Poetry Review, Verse Matters.* 'Bobowler' was commissioned by the BBC and National Poetry Day for *Free The Word*. Italicised lines in 'The Yellow Curtains' are taken from 'The Yellow Wallpaper' by Charlotte Perkins Gilman.